BEGINNINGS

Use one of these two techniques at the beginning of any unit in this book.

Brainstorm:

Make a very large illustration of the topic out of butcher paper. Brainstorm with the children in your classroom all the words that describe or make you think of this topic. Write these words on the butcher paper. Display the chart throughout the unit. Use these words for vocabulary development, alphabetical order, dictionary search, and many other language activities.

This is the very best way to begin any theme or unit of study. You are not only building vocabulary with the students in your classroom, you are also finding out just how much they know about any given topic.

If you don't feel comfortable starting every unit with this exact activity, here is an alternative.

Cooperative Groups:

Divide your class into cooperative groups. Ask each group to come up with as many words as they can think of about the specified topic. Now have the group put those words in alphabetical order. Make a chart using these words in the following manner. Have one representative from each group be the spokesperson. One group at a time will give you the first word on their list. As the facilitator you simply write the word on the chart. Repeat with the second word on each list and so on until all the words have been added to the chart.

Not only is this a great alphabetical order and vocabulary activity, it is also a problem-solving activity. As the children give you their words they will possibly have to re-alphabetize them. Is there enough space to write the word above one that has already been written? Will they see that they have to start anticipating what letter may come next?

Please don't think this is a good activity for older children only. This has been done very successfully with first graders!

After you have finished this activity, display the list of words you have developed.

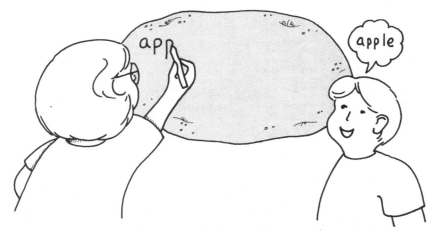

Language Activities to Use With Any Topic

Use any of these activities with your brainstorming charts. Write the appropriate letters, words, phrases, etc. on the blank potato and pig forms provided for you. You will need to make your own popcorn page to use.

Alphabetical Order:

Write the words appropriate for your class on the blank shapes. Have children cut out the shapes and place them in alphabetical order on the top of their desks. Have a partner check the words to be sure they are correct. Only then have the children paste the words along a strip of construction paper. (Use green or brown for a potato patch, brown for a pig pen, and any color for a "popcorn popper.")

Spelling and/or Reading:

Reproduce the blank shape on construction paper. Write one appropriate spelling word on each shape. Place the shapes on the floor around the room. If you have two doors in your classroom that go out into the hall, place the pigs in a circle through the doors. When children are finished with their work, they may get a partner and step on the shapes, reading or spelling the words as they go. You will be amazed at the number of children throughout the school that will have to go by your classroom to get anywhere in the building! You are not only getting the children in your classroom involved, you are involving the whole school!

   • Potatoes • Popcorn • Pigs

Dictionary Skills:

Use the words from the vocabulary chart to work on dictionary skills. Each child is assigned one or more of the words to look up in the dictionary. For oral participation ask children questions such as "What are the guide words?" or "What part of speech is your word?" Then have children write the definition for their word on the appropriate shape. Reproduce the "Bingo" grid on the inside back cover of this book. Have the children choose the words they want from the vocabulary chart for the unit and write one word in each square. This way everyone will have a different card. Instead of calling out the word, read the definition from one of the shapes the children have done.

Listening:

Fill a container with blank shapes containing appropriate words from the brainstorming chart. (Use something fun like a brown paper bag for a potato sack, a bowl or popcorn box for popcorn, or a bucket for hungry pigs.) Each day choose one of the words as the "word of the day." Use this word as many times during the day as possible. When the children hear you use this word they are to yell out the name of the unit you are studying. (POTATO, POPCORN, or PIG) Keep track of how many times they yell out the word at the appropriate time. Reward the class for their good listening at the end of the day.

Centers:

Set up centers to practice activities using the vocabulary from your word banks. These can simply be containers (popcorn boxes, potato sacks, paper bag pig pens) and cards containing words to sort.

Basic Cross-Legged Critter Directions

You will need:

- 9" (22.8 cm) square of construction paper
- scissors
- stapler

1. Fold.

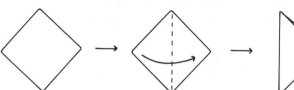

2. Now fold again.

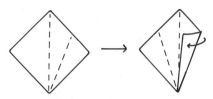

3. Fold the narrow point to the top point.

4. Open the paper. Cut up the center line and the two side lines as shown in the illustration.

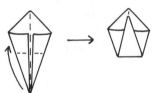

5. Re-fold the paper. Cross the legs and pull the two pocket pieces forward.

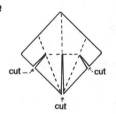

6. Overlap the pocket pieces and the crossed legs. Staple in place. Optional: Trim legs.

foot
pocket (pull out to staple)

Variations:

Use scraps of paper and marking pens to complete these "cross-legged critters."

French Fry Holder  Popcorn Dragon Pig

• Potatoes • Popcorn • Pigs

Celebrating Potatoes

Read about Potatoes:

Non-Fiction

Potatoes by Dorothy Turner; Carolrhoda Books, Inc., 1989.
Potatoe by Barrie Watts; Stopwatch Books, Silver Burdett Press, 1987.
Maps and Globes by Jack Knowlton; Harper and Row, 1985.

Fiction

One Potato by Sue Porter; Bradbury Press, 1989.
Leprechauns Never Lie by Lorna Balian; Abingdon, 1980.

Beginnings--(See pages 1-3 for complete directions.)

Make your large potato from brown butcher paper to create a "Potato Power" word bank. Use this chart for skills such as ...

- Alphabetical Order
- Dictionary Skills
- Spelling
- Listening
- Creative Writing Word Bank

POTATOES

One potato, two potato
Three potato, four
Five potato, six potato
Two rolled out the door.

Seven potato, eight potato
Nine potato, ten
I looked out and there I saw
The lost potato twins.

One was Paul and one was Pete
And they were on their way
To visit more potato pals
On Baked Potato Way.

I didn't know that every year
Potatoes gather round
And celebrate the many ways
Potatoes can be found.

Linda Holliman

GRANDPA AND THE TATER PATCH

My Grandpa planted "taters"
He put them in a row
He watered them and weeded them
To help to make them grow.

My Grandma needed "taters"
To put into her stew
So Grandpa sent me to the garden
I knew just what to do.

I started digging "taters"
I couldn't seem to quit
I dug up ALL of the "taters"
And Grandpa threw a fit!

Linda Holliman

Potatoes...They're Academic

"Spud" Concentration:

Give each child a brown paper lunch bag and a page of blank potatoes. Have them write one spelling word or reading vocabulary word on each potato. They practice these words during the week. One way to practice is to play "concentration" with a partner.

Take both sets of potato cards and lay them face down. The first player picks up one card and reads it. He/She then tries to select a matching potato. If the second card matches the first, the player keeps the card and plays again. If there is no match, both cards are turned back over and another child takes a turn.

Contractions:

Make French Fry Holders. (See page 3.) Write the contraction on the front of the French fry holder and then write the words that make up the contraction on French fries cut from yellow construction paper. Have the children put the correct French fries into the correct holder to make the contraction.

Syllabication:

Potato vocabulary words can be used for teaching syllabication. Make three potato plants on your bulletin board. Label the plants 1 syllable, 2 syllables, and 3 syllables. Cut out some potatoes from brown construction paper and write a potato word on each one. Make sure the words have one, two, or three syllables. At the bottom of the potato plants put the correct number of pins to correspond with the number of potatoes that fit that number of syllables. Place the potatoes in a can or a brown paper bag. Children read the words and place them on a pin under the correct potato plant.

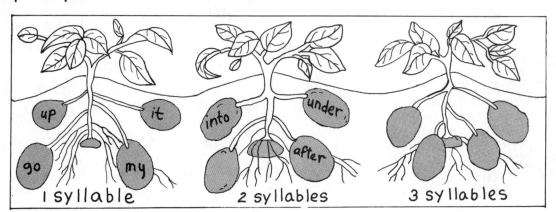

The bulletin board on the preceding page can be adapted to sort parts of speech and identify plural forms.

Parts of Speech:
Write nouns, verbs, and adjectives on the blank potatoes and label the potato plants accordingly. Have the children attach the correct word to the correct potato plant.

Plural Forms:
Label the potato plants for correct plurals (s, es, or ies). Discuss how each plural is formed. Write singular words on the potatoes. Children read the cards and match each word to the correct ending to make it a plural.

Three-Fold Potato Book
Each student needs a 12" X 18" (30.5 x 45.7 cm) piece of brown construction paper and a sheet of writing paper.

1. Fold the brown paper into thirds.

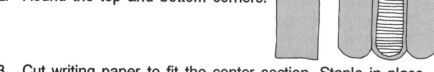

2. Round the top and bottom corners.

3. Cut writing paper to fit the center section. Staple in place.

4. Write about potatoes. For example:

   "My Favorite Potato Recipe"
   An original story about a potato adventure
   A report containing interesting true facts about potatoes
   Copy a favorite potato poem in your best handwriting.

   Peel them,   Fry them,
   Dice them,   Mash them,
   Put them in a pan.   I'm a potato fan!

   by *Linda Holliman*

 • Potatoes • Popcorn • Pigs

Potato People

Create them! Write about them!

THINK of a famous person to turn into a "Potato Person" you could take on an adventure. (Children can also make "potato pets" using the same materials.)

THEN...Transform a real potato into a potato person. OR...(if you want your potato person to last) make it out of panty hose, brown butcher paper, or clay. Let the children in your classroom choose which kind they want to make.

Panty Hose Potato People:

Cut a panty hose leg about 6 inches long. Tie a knot in one end. Turn the panty hose inside out (so that the knot is now on the inside). Stuff the potato and tie another knot at the end. Provide yarn, paint, buttons, lace, etc. for children to use in creating their potato people.

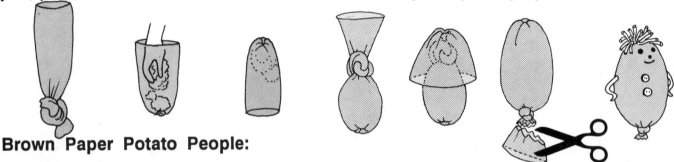

Brown Paper Potato People:

Give your potato person a three-dimensional effect by cutting two pieces of brown paper, stapling about 2/3 of the way around the edges and stuffing it with scraps of paper or tissue. Staple the rest of the way around and have the children decorate their potato to become the person they want it to be. Decorate the potato before you stuff it.

Clay Potato People:

Brown clay or playdough will make perfect potato people also.

NOW...Have children write about their potato people.

- Where do they like to live?
- What do they eat?
- What is their favorite sport, T.V. show, movie, color, etc.?

Older students can write an adventure for their potato person.

FINALLY...Display your potato person.

Display potato people and stories in dioramas or on a class bulletin board display. Be sure they include their potato person in correct clothing for the climate and adventure.

8   • Potatoes • Popcorn • Pigs

BOOK PROJECT---*Leprechauns Never Lie* by Lorna Balian

This delightful book set in Ireland can be used to teach or review a variety of skills.

Sequencing--Read the story aloud to your students. Then have them recall the order of the jobs the leprechaun convinced Ninny Nanny to do as she searched for treasure.

Discuss the Story--Encourage discussion of events and characters in the story by asking questions such as these.

- What words would you use to describe Ninny nanny's character?
- What words would you use to describe the leprechaun?
- Was the leprechaun alwayds telling the truth? Explain your answer.
- What did Gram want Ninny Nanny to do?
- Can you explain what the leprechaun did for Ninny Nanny?
- What did you learn about Ireland from hearing this story?

Vocabulary Development--There are many words in this story that the children in your classroom may not be familiar with. Work together to create a list of these words. Use them for practicing synonyms and antonyms, dictionary skills, or as your spelling words. Encourage children to use the words when creating their own stories about Ireland, Leprechauns, and potatoes.

fetch	nestled	naught	boasted
grubbed	glen	blathering	tramping
heap	ailing	dawdled	wee
scattered	britches	shrieked	pitching
disgust	hissed	mite	stray
bawled	mumbled	wobbled	squawked
vanished	hasty	foolish	bound

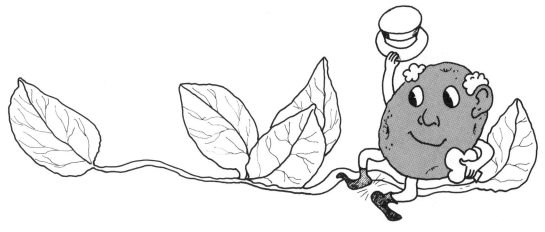

9 • Potatoes • Popcorn • Pigs

POTATO MATH

Have each child in your classroom bring a potato to school and the math fun begins!

Graphing--Graph the different kinds of potatoes the children bring to school.

NEW POTATOES
YAMS
SWEET POTATOES
RUSSET
BAKING POTATOES

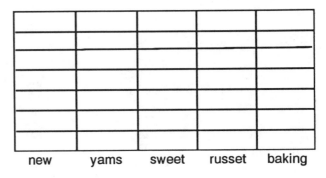

new	yams	sweet	russet	baking

Graph the favorite ways to eat potatoes...

FRENCH FRIES
BAKED
TATER TOTS
POTATO CHIPS
POTATO SOUP
MASHED

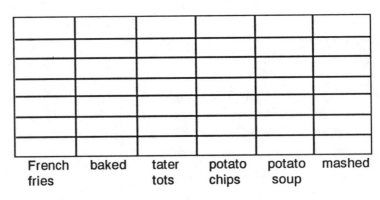

French fries	baked	tater tots	potato chips	potato soup	mashed

Counting--Make French fries from yellow sponges for counting!

Take a yellow sponge and cut it into strips.

Make a French fry holder from your basic cross-legged critter pattern. (See page 4.) Round off the top and fold the legs back. Put a number on the front and start counting!

To use your French fry holders to teach or practice subtraction, make your French fries from yellow construction paper. Write the math problems on the French fries and have the child put the correct French fry in the correct holder.

• Potatoes • Popcorn • Pigs

Estimation--Get a 10-pound sack of potatoes. Have children look at one of the potatoes to give them some basic size information before they try to answer these questions. (Be sure to check answers by doing the activity listed.)

How many potatoes are in an average 10-pound bag? (You may want to use three different bags to check the answer.)

How many French fries can you get from an average potato?

How many potatoes does it take to make two cups of mashed potatoes?

What to do with a 10-pound bag of potatoes:

Now that you have all of those potatos, how about finding out this information...

- Find the shortest.
- Find the longest.
- Find the bumpiest.
- Find the smoothest.
- Find the smallest.
- Find the largest.
- Find the potato that weighs the least.
- Find the potato that weighs the most.
- Find two potatoes that weigh the same. Do they look the same?

If you have older students, continue potato math by doing the following...

Divide your students into groups. Give each group a lunch bag of potatoes. Have a scale available for weighing the potatoes. Have them discover ...

How much does your sack of potatoes weigh?
How many potatoes are in the sack of potatoes?
Find the average weight of a potato.
Weigh each potato. Do any weigh the average amount?

     • Potatoes • Popcorn • Pigs

POTATO FACTS

Potatoes came from South America, but they came the long way round to get to North America. The explorer, Francisco Pizzaro, took potatoes back to Spain. When Spanish colonists settled in Florida, they brought potatoes to North America with them. British adventurers took potatoes back home where the British farmers planted them as food for hogs and cattle. The Irish make potatoes a large part of their diet. When the Irish settlers came to America, they planted potatoes as food.

Using a world map, have the children in your classroom trace the path that the potato took to get to the United States. This is the perfect opportunity to teach or practice map skills. Even very young children can get an idea of how to use a map and to recognize countries.

You may want to have individual children or cooperative learning groups trace the route of the potato. Give each child or group a copy of the world map on the following page. Have them trace the route with crayons or marking pens.

 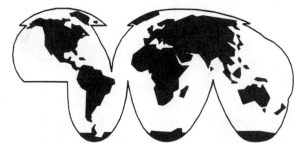

Create questions about the history of potatoes that are appropriate to the age and ability of your students. For example:

1. Study Ireland during your potato unit. Discover what happened during the Irish Potato Famine.

2. How does the potato pancake fit into the Jewish celebration of Hanukkah?

3. How are potatoes grown and harvested in our country today?

"Potato Facts..."

Have your students write facts on the blank potato forms. You can have older students practice using the various sentence forms by writing one fact in three different ways. For example:

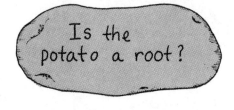 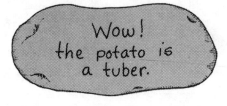 

• Potatoes • Popcorn • Pigs

Directions:

Trace the route of the potato from the New World to the Old World and back again.

13   • Potatoes • Popcorn • Pigs

SCIENCE

Grow a Sweet Potato:

Stick three or four toothpicks in the side of an old sweet potato that has been in a dark place and started to sprout a little. Put it in a clear glass with the toothpicks resting on the rim. Fill the jar with water and put the sweet potato in the sunlight and watch it grow. Be patient... it may take a while to start growing.

Take this activity a step further by having children observe plant growth and record what they see. This can be done with the whole class observing one potato or have each child bring a potato from home and let them compare the growth of a variety of potatoes.

Make a large chart for class observation or individual charts for each child. Observe and record the amount of water used, the height of the plant, and the growth pattern of the leaves. This is a good opportunity to practice measuring.

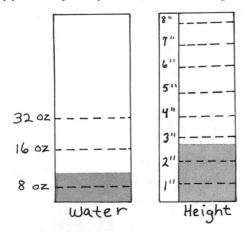

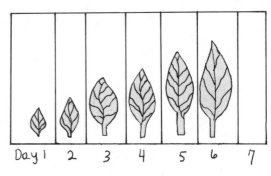

Other "Potato" Experiments:

Over a period of a few months do the following experiments. (These can be done as a whole class activity or in cooperative learning groups.) Take two potato plants that are similar in size and development for each experiment.

- Feed one of the potatoes with plant fertilizer and observe and record differences in growth that might take place.

- Put one of the potatoes in sunlight and the other in the dark. Observe and record what happens.

These activities can be used to show children what is involved in a science project before they are asked to develop their own science fair projects. You are modeling the correct sequence of an experiment, plus observation and recording skills.

GROW A MR. POTATO HEAD

Have each child in your classroom bring a large potato to school. Cut off one end of the potato so it will sit flat. Scoop out the other end of the potato. Line the scooped out end with absorbent cotton or blotting paper and stand the potato in a small bowl of water. Sprinkle grass seed into the scooped out end and keep it watered. In a few days your Mr. Potato will be growing green hair. Add a face with buttons or cloves or construction paper. As the "hair" grows, it can be cut and shaped into various styles.

Cooking Potatoes--What does cooking do to a potato?

Observe potatoes before, during, and after cooking to complete these statements...

Before cooking a potato is _____.

After boiling a potato is _____.

After frying a potato is _____ on the outside and _____ on the inside.

What happens to a potato slice if it is left sitting in the air?
Can you find out why this happens?

• Potatoes • Popcorn • Pigs

Life Cycle of the Potato Plant

Have each child in your classroom make a POP-UP book to represent the life cycle of the potato. Use the pictures that have been provided on the following page. On the last pop-up, have the children draw their favorite way to eat potatoes.

Directions for pop-up pages: (Make as many as you need.)

1. Take a sheet of paper. Fold it in half and cut as shown.

2. Fold the tab back and forth several times.

3. Open the paper and push the tab to the reverse side.

4. Paste a picture to the tab. (Put the paste on the tab, not the picture.)

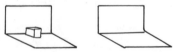

Follow these directions to bind the book together:

1. Glue the pictures back to back being careful not to get glue too near the tab. Add a blank page to the front and to the back to serve as end papers.

2. Cut a cover from colored paper (or tag) slightly larger than the pop-up pages. Score the center and fold. Rub firmly.

3. Paste the end papers to the cover.

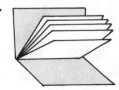

Life Cycle of the Potato

1.

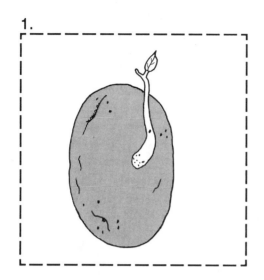

2.

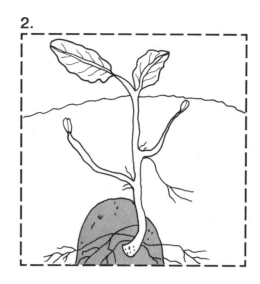

3.

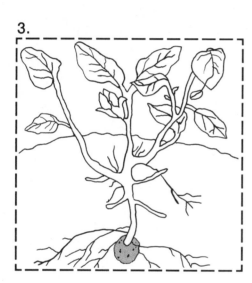

4.

5.

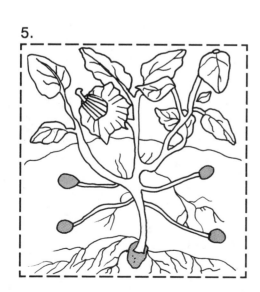

6. (Draw your favorite way to eat potatoes.)

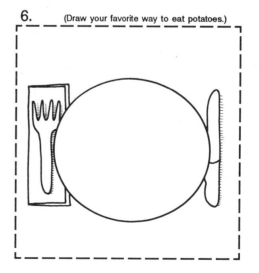

17

• Potatoes • Popcorn • Pigs

BE A POSITIVE POTATO!

Always reinforce positive behavior as you catch children being good. We know that children respond to this much better than negative attention. Use your theme or unit of study to reinforce good behavior. The following are just a few ways to do this using potatoes.

"Positive French Fries"–Have each child make a French fry holder from red construction paper. (Use the basic Cross-legged Critter pattern on page 4.)

Cut a lot of construction paper or sponge French fries and reward good behavior by putting fries in childrens' holders. (When a child earns five or ten French fries, reward them!)

Make your sponge French fries by cutting yellow sponges into strips. They look almost good enough to eat!

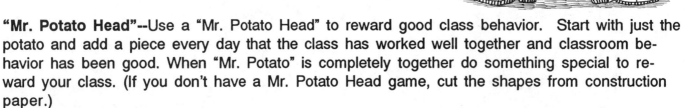

"Mr. Potato Head"--Use a "Mr. Potato Head" to reward good class behavior. Start with just the potato and add a piece every day that the class has worked well together and classroom behavior has been good. When "Mr. Potato" is completely together do something special to reward your class. (If you don't have a Mr. Potato Head game, cut the shapes from construction paper.)

"Positive Potato Sacks"–Give each child a brown lunch sack. Make lots of potatoes from brown construction paper. Put one in a child's sack each time you see that he/she has a positive attitude. You will be so pleased with the positive and precious personalities popping up!

When a child receives ten potatoes, reward this positive behavior with a coupon for French fries at your closest fast food restaurant. (You might get some coupons donated...give it a try.)

• Potatoes • Popcorn • Pigs

ENDINGS

There are many fun ways to bring a unit to an end. The following are just a few.

Write a song!--"I Heard It Through The Grapevine" can easily be adapted to "I Heard It In The Potato Patch" or "Lumpy Has Finally Met His Match." (Please send me a copy of your song. I love to hear what creative students and teachers are doing.)

"Potato" costumes--Creative costumes are easy to make using large brown paper bags.

Baked Potato Party--Everyone in class brings a potato to school. (Ask the cafeteria ahead of time if they will bake the potatoes.) Send home a note asking parents to send a topping for the baked potato party. Have children brainstorm to list the wide variety of possible toppings. There are no wrong answers to this activity. Try to keep the choices as nutritious as possible. On the last day of your potato unit, set up a Potato Bar in class and have lunch together. Make potato-shaped placemats or potato-printed placemats to eat on. (See directions below.)

If you don't want to prepare an entire lunch, have the children bring a potato to class and make potato soup in a crock pot. Have each child peel and cut up their own potato. Cook the potatoes, add salt, pepper, and milk and serve the homemade soup as an afternoon snack.

If you enjoy cooking in your classroom, *Cup Cooking* by Barbara Johnson and Betty Plemons is a great book to have. They give you many recipes such as potato salad that the children make individually.

Potato Printing--Party Place Mats

This simple art activity is a great way to use up some of those potatoes you have around after so many potato activities. Cut the pattern in your potato free-hand with a kitchen knife (be careful!) or use cookie cutters. Press the cookie cutter into the potato and then cut around the print to make your raised pattern for printing. Put tempera in flat dishes. (Paper plates make clean-up quick and easy.) Children dip their designs into the tempera and on to a sheet of construction paper. (If you are using potatoes as part of your unit for St. Patrick's Day, cut shamrocks on your potatoes and use green paint.)

Use these potatoes for projects in this book.

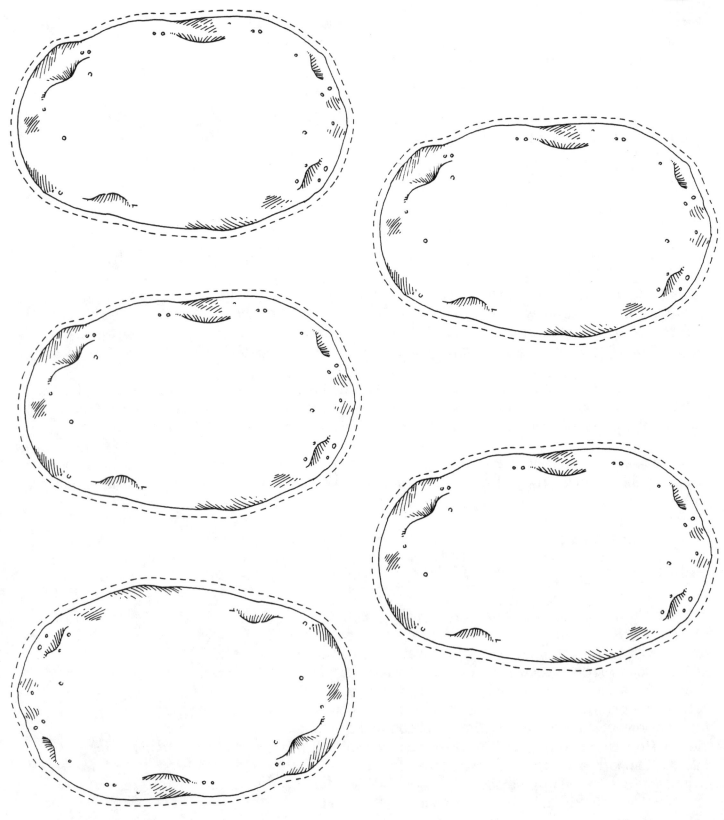

• Potatoes • Popcorn • Pigs

Celebrating Popcorn

Read about Popcorn:

Fiction

The Popcorn Dragon by Jane Thayer; Morrow Junior Books, 1953.
Popcorn by Frank Asch; Parents' Magazine Press, 1979.

Non-Fiction

The Popcorn Book by Tomie de Paola; Scholastic Books, 1978.
CORN: What it is. What it does. by Cynthia Kellogg; Greenwillow Books, 1989.
Corn is Maize, The Gift of the Indians by Aliki; Harper Trophy, 1976.
Science Fun with Peanuts and Popcorn by Rose Wyler; Julian Messner, 1986.

Beginnings--(See pages 1-3 for complete directions.)

Make your large popcorn shape from white butcher paper to create a "Popcorn Is..." word bank. Use this chart for skills such as:

- Alphabetical Order
- Dictionary Skills
- Spelling
- Listening
- Creative Writing Word Bank

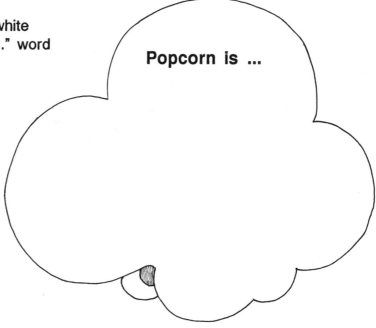

Popcorn is ...

Put in the oil.
Fill up the pot.
Plop go the kernels.
Now, wait until it's hot!

Pop goes the first kernel.
Pop goes the next.
Then pop, pop...explosion.
There go all the rest!

Linda Holliman

Popcorn at the movies.
Popcorn at the game.
Popcorn just for snacking.
Popcorn's not the same!

Now it comes in flavors,
Caramel, nacho cheese.
I love all the flavors.
Pass the popcorn please!

Linda Holliman

LANGUAGE

Compound Words:

Cut popped popcorn out of white and kernels out of yellow construction paper. Write the compound word on the popped popcorn. Write one half of the compound word on one kernel and the other half on a second kernel. Children match up words on the popcorn kernels to make the compound word. After they have matched all the words they can check themselves by matching the kernels to the popped, corn words.

Make a sheet of blank popped popcorn shapes. Write one word on each piece of popcorn. (Use both correct and incorrect compound words.) Ask the children to color the correct compound words one color and the incorrect words another color. This becomes a good review for the children and is very easy to check.

Vowels:

Make a sheet of blank popped popcorn. Select popcorn words from your chart that have short vowel sounds in them (snack, Indian, pop, cob, yellow, stick, butter, etc.). Write one of the words in each of the blank popcorn shapes. Make sure you have every short vowel sound represented. Now make a large construction paper popcorn bowl for each short vowel sound. Make each bowl a different color. Label each bowl. Have the children color the popcorn on their sheets the correct colors to correspond with the bowls. Put the children in cooperative learning groups to check their work with each other. Then have them cut out the popcorn and glue each piece into the correct bowl. This makes a great hallway display or bulletin board.

   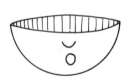 

Proper Nouns:

Popcorn is a great way to practice recognizing proper nouns. Prepare a bowl of popped corn and a bowl of unpopped kernels. Give each child a card containing a sentence or short paragraph. Be sure to double or even triple space the paragraph so there will be room for the popcorn. Have the child glue a popped corn piece under each word that needs a capital letter (proper noun) and an unpopped kernel under each word that does not need a capital. For example:

> We went to Oakland, California on a trip.

22

• Potatoes • Popcorn • Pigs

Names:

Use popcorn to help very young children are just beginning to write their names. This activity helps reinforce capital and lower case letters. Write each child's name on a piece of colored poster board. Leave space between each letter to accommodate the popcorn that will be glued on the letters. Have the children glue popped corn on the capital letters of their names and popcorn kernels on the lower case letters. Save these for an Open House display. Be sure to have extra popcorn for the children to eat. Could you resist the temptation?

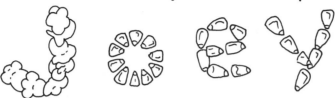

Subject and Predicate:

Make a sheet of blank popped corn shapes. Write subjects on half of the blank popcorn and predicates on the other half. Have children color the subjects yellow and the predicates orange. They then cut out the popcorn pieces and match a yellow to an orange to create complete sentences about popcorn. You may want to make a giant popcorn bowl chart where each child can glue one of his/her completed sentences.

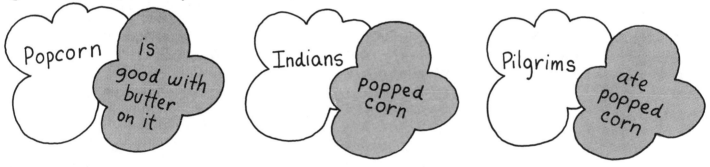

Share Books:

Give everyone in your class an opportunity to read and then share a book in this very special way. Give everyone a white or brown lunch sack. Have them write the title, author, and illustrator on one side, and on the other side draw a picture of an important scene in the book. While the children are working on this, you pop the POPCORN! Fill everyone's sack with popcorn, sit in a circle, and let everyone share their books as they enjoy the popcorn. When everyone has had a turn, you can extend the activity by having them write about the part in their book that was most like popcorn and tell why.

Don't throw those sacks away...make a display on the bulletin board with them. Have the children write the popcorn part of their book on a piece of popped popcorn and put that inside the sack. When they have time to "read the room" after their work is completed, they can pull the popcorn out of the sack and read.

"Popcorn" Reading:

To encourage reading in your classroom, give children credit for minutes or pages read rather than books read. For some children it is almost overwhelming to read a whole book. By rewarding minutes or pages, all children can be successful and see their own progress.

This activity can be done two ways.

1. Bring a jar to school and a bag of popcorn kernels. For every ten minutes a child reads, drop a kernel in the jar. When the jar is full there should certainly be some kind of wonderful popcorn reward. Maybe you have a mom that would make popcorn balls for your class. Or show a movie (with popcorn of course). Know your class and what they would enjoy and be willing to work for.

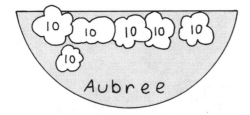
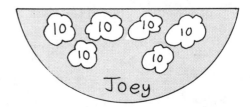

2. This idea can also be adapted to work with individual students. Make each of your students a bowl out of construction paper. When they have completed reading for one specified time or have read ten pages, give them a piece of popped popcorn and glue it in their popcorn bowl. Determine with the child what his/her reward will be when the bowl is full.

Pop the Question--Research Skills

Ask popcorn questions to encourage children to use the encyclopedia, almanac and other research tools. For example, pop on over to your library and try to find the answers to these questions.

Who is Orville Redenbocker?

How much popcorn is consumed in the United States?

Where is the most popcorn eaten in the United States?

• Potatoes • Popcorn • Pigs

BOOK PROJECT--*The Popcorn Book* by Tomie de Paola

The Popcorn Book by Tomie de Paola is an excellent book to use at the beginning of your popcorn unit. There is so much information in it that can be incorporated into a social studies and science unit. It also gives you and your children some wonderful facts to discuss and verify.

The Indian legend about why the popcorn pops is fascinating to children and can be used to encourage creative writing.

Give each child a piece of 9" x 12" (22.9 X 30.5 cm) white construction paper. Fold it in half. With the fold at the bottom, fold down the top piece of paper. Draw a popped popcornshape on the front of the folded piece of paper. On the inside have the children draw what they think is inside the kernel of the popcorn that makes it pop. After the drawing is done, have the children create a new legend about why the popcorn pops.

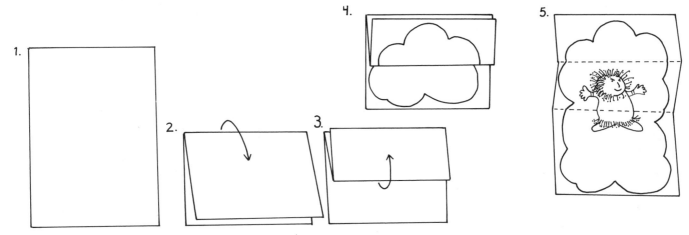

You can also incorporate popcorn myths and legends into a Tall Tale unit. Read the legend in *The Popcorn Book* to your class, then have them create their own tall tales about popcorn.

- The Day it Rained Popcorn
- The Day it Was so Hot all the Popcorn in the Fields Popped
- The "Popcorn" Touch

BOOK PROJECT--*The Popcorn Dragon* by Jane Thayer

This is an old book that has been reprinted with new illustrations. There are several ways you can use this book in your popcorn unit. The children will enjoy the antics of the dragon and there will be lessons to learn!

1. After reading this book to the children in your classroom, discuss what the qualities of a good friend are. Have the children list what they think are good qualities.

2. Make a large dragon in the center of a bulletin board. Give each child a piece of popcorn shaped paper and have them write one quality of a good friend. Place the popcorn around the dragon.

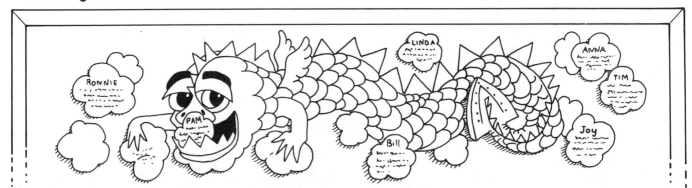

3. Make green dragons out of the basic Cross-legged Critter pattern. (See page 4.) Simply add a dragon head and a long scaly tail. For a three-dimensional look, pin these dragons on a bulletin board and have the children put their friend's qualities in the pockets of the dragons. Have them write them on popcorn of course!

4. When you are bringing your popcorn unit to an end, take the three-dimensional dragons down and fill them with popcorn. Spend some time reviewing all the activities you did with popcorn. You may even want to graph the five best activities. The children can enjoy eating popcorn and remembering all the wonderful things they learned.

5. Another way you can use *The Popcorn Dragon* is to teach or review the "wh" sound. There is a lot of smoke blowing in this story, and the dragon used that sound a lot! Have the children make lists of words that begin with the "wh" sound or have that sound in the word. Use the bulletin board ideas in number 1 or 2 to display those words that your class has found.

 • Potatoes • Popcorn • Pigs

POPCORN MATH

Computation:

In the fall of the year when you are teaching number recognition, addition, subtraction, or multiplication, use colored popcorn kernels in a center to practice those skills. Divide a piece of white construction paper into about six spaces. Draw a tree in each space. Write a math fact below each tree. Have the child answer the problem by gluing the correct number of pieces of colored popcorn on each fall tree. (Since this could look like leaves on a fall tree, make sure younger students understand that popcorn doesn't really grow on trees.)

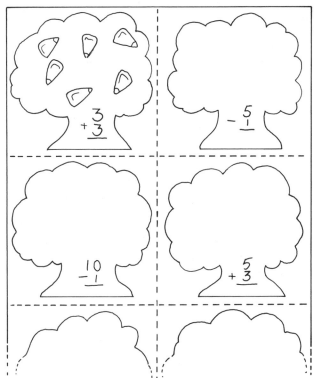

Place Value:

Use popped popcorn to represent the tens and kernels to represent the ones. Give each child a sheet of numbers and have them glue on the popcorn to represent the number.

34

52

19

Graphing:

Use popcorn for a graphing activity. There are so many different flavors of popcorn now that you can have a tasting party and then graph the favorite flavors. You might try using only four flavors (regular, caramel, cheese and nacho, for example). Place four bowls in front of the graph. Have a small group at a time come up and taste the popcorn. Have popcorn squares already available for the children to place on the graph to represent their favorite flavor. When everyone has had the opportunity to choose their favorite flavor, have the children help you glue the squares down. Give each child in your classroom a sheet of graph paper and have them record the information off the large graph.

Older children can then make up story problems from the information on the graph. Choose one problem from each child for math on the following day. Children love to read their own names and names of their classmates in story problems.

Counting to 100:

Count out 100 kernels of popcorn and have the children predict how many of the kernels will pop. Pop the popcorn. Cool it and count how many kernels did pop and how many kernels did not pop. How close did your students come to the correct number? (You can use this same activity to practice fractions or percentages with older students.)

Math with Colored Popcorn:

Estimate the Number--Bring a jar of colored popcorn into your classroom. Show several kernels to your students so that they have an idea of size. Then have your students estimate how many kernels are in the jar. Record their answers on a "piece of popcorn" made of white butcher paper. Unless your class has had a lot of experience with estimating, they will be very surprised at how far they are from the real number.

Count the Contents--Divide the contents of the jar among the children in your classroom. Have each group count and make a tally of the colors of their popcorn. Then make a master list of the numbers of each color from all of the groups. (Here is some great addition practice!) Have them compare the total number of all colors to see how close their estimate was to the real number.

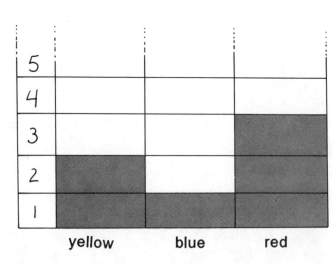

Graph the Colors--Have each group create a graph (using one-inch graph paper) of their share of the popcorn. Combine all of their "counts" on a total class graph. (Have older children create a pie graph instead of a bar graph.)

Measurement:

Take 20 unpopped kernels and 20 popped kernels for the following measurement activities.

1. **Length**--"Which will be the longest line, the unpopped or the popped popcorn?" Lay out the kernels and measure to see if your estimate was correct.

2. **Volume**--"Which do you think fills more spoonfuls, the unpopped popcorn or the popped popcorn?" Use a teaspoon and measure to see which is more.

       • Potatoes • Popcorn • Pigs

SOCIAL STUDIES

There are three types of corn. There is field corn, which we use to feed animals; sweet corn, which we eat; and the oldest form, popcorn.

Popcorn was discovered by the Indians in the Americas many thousands of years ago. When Columbus sailed into San Salvador while exploring the New World, one of the first sights he saw was the Indians selling popcorn and wearing it for jewelry.

Three-Fold Popcorn Books:

Give every child in your classroom three pieces of popcorn shaped writing paper. Have them make a three-fold book in the shape of popped popcorn (see directions below), and assign them to find at least three facts about each kind of corn. These facts are to be written on their popcorn pages and stapled into their three-fold books.

1. Take a 6" X 18" (15.24 X 45.7 cm) sheet of white construction paper.

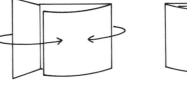

2. Fold the paper into thirds and cut as shown.

3. Staple the popcorn writing paper inside the book.

Other research questions you might use:

- What states grow the most popcorn?
- Who buys the most popcorn/sweet corn/field corn?
- How did the Indians pop corn?
- In what ways did they eat corn?
- How did the colonists first eat popcorn?

You can study popcorn as a unit of its own or incorporate it into such social study units as Native Americans, Colonial Period, or Columbus' Discoveries in the New World.

 • Potatoes • Popcorn • Pigs

SCIENCE

The Indian legend in Tomie de Paola's popcorn book provides the perfect opportunity to talk to your class about what is really inside a kernel of popcorn that makes it pop!

A lot of water is sealed inside a kernel of popcorn. When you heat the popcorn, the water inside gets very hot and turns to steam. The steam takes up more and more space inside the popcorn. The steam finally takes up so much room that the kernel splits. The steam shoots out and the air rushes in and that is what makes the popcorn so light and fluffy.

What happens if...?

If popcorn needs moisture to pop, then what would happen if you soaked the kernels in water overnight? Ask your class this question and have the children predict the answer. Then soak the kernels and see what happens. It will be interesting to the children to see the outcome. After you have done this ask the children why they think the popcorn didn't pop.

Sink or Float:

Use popcorn to teach the concept of sink or float. If you put a kernel of popcorn into a glass of water, it will sink. If you put a popped piece of popcorn into water, it will float. Discuss with your class why something sinks or floats. Popped popcorn is less dense, lighter than water while kernels are heavier than water. Have children find other items that will float and other items that will sink in water. Try other liquids, such as fruit juice and syrup. Is the result the same?

Good Behavior--Popcorn Style!

There are many days in the classroom when we feel as though we are in the hot pot with 20 to 30 kernels hot and poppin about the room. The following is a suggestion to keep them popping in the right direction.

Make each child in your classroom a popcorn bowl from colored construction paper. Make up a bunch of popped popcorn shapes from white construction paper. Add a piece of this popcorn to a child's bowl when he/she is poppin good!

When children have five (or any number you set in advance) pieces of popcorn in their bowl, send them home with a small bag of popcorn.

ENDINGS

Pop Goes the Popcorn!

End your celebration of popcorn with this activity. It is a favorite among children of all ages! Discuss the safety rules when making hot popcorn and then have fun watching the popcorn pop!

Spread out a sheet in the middle of your classroom floor. Place the popcorn popper without its lid in the middle of the sheet. Have the children sit around the edge of the sheet. (Be sure to maintain a safe distance from the popper.) Remind them of the safety rules you have already gone over and let the popping begin!

Seeing the popcorn pop all over the sheet is fun and shows the children the importance of keeping the lid on when popping corn at home. When the corn has finished popping, everyone can dig in for a final popcorn treat. (Have extra already popped so everyone can be satisfied.)

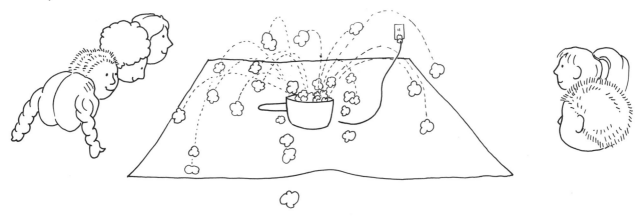

• Potatoes • Popcorn • Pigs

Celebrating Pigs

"Pig Out" on Good Books

The Amazing Pig by Paul Galdone; Clarion, 1981.
Apple Pigs by Ruth Orbach; Putnam, 1981.
Charlotte's Web by E. B. White; Harper, 1952.
Emmett's Pig by Mary Stolz; Harper and Row, 1959.
Mr. and Mrs. Pig's Night Out by Mary Raynor; MacMillan, 1976.
Mud Baths for Everyone by Denys Cazet; Willowisp Press, 1986.
The Piggy in the Puddle by Charlotte Pomerantz; MacMillan, 1974.
Pig's in Hiding by Arlene Dubanevich; MacMillan, 1983.
The "Pig Pig" Books by David McPhail; Dutton
The Three Little Pigs by Erick Blegvad; MacMillan, 1980.
The Three Little Pigs by Joseph Jacobs; Putnam, 1980.
A Treeful of Pigs by Anita Lobel; Scholastic, 1988.
The True Story of the Three Pigs as Told by A. Wolf by Jon Scieszko; Viking Kestral, 1989.

Beginnings--(See pages 1-3 for complete directions.)

Make your large pig from pink butcher
paper to create a "Pigs Are..." word bank.
Use this chart for skills such as:

- Alphabetical Order
- Dictionary Skills
- Spelling
- Listening
- Creative Writing Word Bank

Beginnings--Setting the Stage

Set the stage in your classroom for "Hog Wild Happenings" and "Sow Celebrations" by making one corner of your room into a pig pen. Cut out a cardboard fence to section off the pig pen. Add pillows and a trough with lots of pig books and you will be off to a good start. Include fiction and non-fiction in the trough. Add some stuffed pigs from home. Look for pig jigsaw puzzles to include in the pig pen.

If a cardboard fence is not possible, make one out of brown butcher paper and attach it to the wall. This will work as well to display the books and puzzles you have gathered for your Pig Week celebration.

                                       • Potatoes • Popcorn • Pigs

"Personality Pigs"

This activity has always been one of the most popular with the children in my classroom.

1. Create your "Personality Pig"--Give each child in your classroom a 12" x 18" (30.5 x 45.7 cm) piece of bright pink construction paper. The children may use markers, crayons, and pieces of construction paper in a variety of colors to create their "Personality Pig" (Statue of Liberty pig, chef pig, sports pig, super hero pig, etc.).

2. The next step is to develop the character. Give your pig an interesting name. Think about what he/she likes and dislikes. What does your Personality Pig like to eat? What is his/her favorite T.V. show, book, color, hobby? What does he/she really hate? When you know all about your pig's character write...

   • a paragraph describing him/her
   • an exciting adventure for him/her
   • an interview with him/her

An alternative to this activity would be to put the names of all the "Personality Pigs" in a sack. Have every child draw someone else's pig. Now be creative and write about the pig you have drawn. Don't give the name of the pig, but make your description so clear the other children can guess who you are writing about.

Or work in cooperative groups and take all of the pigs in your group on an adventure. You may like your "Personality Pigs" so much that you will want to write many stories about them throughout the year.

 **"The Piggy Times"--Write a Newspaper**
"Hooterville Hoggers beat Summerville Sows 29 to 7."

Putting together a newspaper is a good learning experience for the children in your classroom. Use your "Personality Pigs" as the basis for articles in the newspaper. Let everyone have the opportunity to be both Pig and reporter for writing stories and interviews about these delightful "porkers." Be sure to include book reviews, ads, cartoons, sports, and of course a society page.

 • Potatoes • Popcorn • Pigs

Bulletin Boards that Teach

Feed the Pigs:

Make a series of troughs or pig pens across your bulletin board. Run off the blank pig patterns in this unit on pink construction paper. Use the pigs to sort the correct information into the correct fence or trough. These may be used for practicing skills in any academic area with just a little imagination on your part. For example:

Categorization--Write the name of each category to be practiced on a trough or pen. Write the names of items in each category on the blank pig forms. Children sort the pigs and place them in the correct trough or pen. Some categories you might use are...

toys	pets	clothing
animals	vegetables	minerals
birds	mammals	insects
people	places	things

Parts of Speech--If you are reviewing parts of speech, each trough or pen can be labeled with the parts of speech you are practicing (noun, verb, preposition, etc.). The pigs would contain a variety of words that could be placed in the correct trough or pen.

Math--Label each trough or pen with a numeral. Write problems on each blank pig. Children solve the problem and place the pig in the correct trough or pen.

Poetry

Here are two perfect pig poems for your "Pig Week" celebration.

Use this old favorite for handwriting practice and as an art experience.

This little piggy went to the market,
This little piggy stayed home,
This little piggy had roast beef,
This little piggy had none,
And this little piggy went wee-wee-wee
All the way home!

Give each child a piece of construction paper and a sheet of writing paper both cut in the shape of a large foot. Each child copies the poem in his/her best handwriting and staples it to the paper foot. Turn each "toe" into a little piggy by simply adding a snout, eyes, ears, and a tail with paper scraps and crayons.

This humorous pig poem works with children of all ages. It's a perfect addition to a Whole Language approach to your "Pig Week" celebration.

I had a little pig,
I fed him in a trough,
He got so fat
His tail dropped off.
So I got me a hammer,
And I got me a nail,
And I made my little pig
A brand-new tail.

Anonymous

Put the poem on a chart and have everyone read it together several times. Leave the poem hanging somewhere in the room for the children to read again and again. Then bring out the paper plates and have every child make their own little pig. (See directions on the following page.)

This pig poem also makes a wonderful display for the hall or on a bulletin board. Copy the poem on a large piece of paper and surround it with all the little piggies with the brand new tails.

       • Potatoes • Popcorn • Pigs

Paper Plate Pigs

Each child will need:

- a paper plate (no wax on plates)
- crayons
- pink construction paper (8 1/2" x 11") (21.6 x 28 cm)
- scraps of brown construction paper

1. Color the paper plate pink.

2. Use a black crayon to draw on a snout and eyes.

3. Cut pink head, feet, and ears from the pink construction paper.

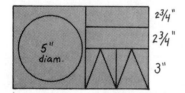

5" diam.   2¾"   2¾"   3"

4. Give each child a piece of brown construction paper to make their little pig a brand new tail. Don't forget to include the "nails" on the new tail!

• Potatoes • Popcorn • Pigs

Pig Limericks

Pigericks by Arnold Lobel is the perfect way to introduce the children in your classroom to limericks. Read *Pigericks* to your class and discuss the pattern found in each limerick. Get the children to identify the pattern. Make a model of this pattern for them on the chalkboard or on a chart. This will give them something to work from and to refer to when they start writing their own.

Writing a Limerick:

Line 1--a
Line 2--a
Line 3--b
Line 4--b
Line 5--a

1. Create your first line. You may want to follow a pattern, such as "There was a pig named _____,"or "There once was a pig from _____."

2. Make a list of words that rhyme with the last word in your first line. Use these words to help you as you write line two and line five.

3. Think of a second line that rhymes with your first line.

4. Write two short lines that rhyme which tell about your pig.

5. Now think of a final line that rhymes with your first line. (You may want to repeat part of your first line following the pattern "That pig named _____," or "That pig from _____").

6. Write your whole limerick on a sheet of paper. Illustrate it.

Remember when starting anything new with the children in your classroom to model the exact procedure you want them to follow. Do several of the activities as a class and only then set them loose in small groups or individually.

Display the finished limericks in your class so others may enjoy them.

• Potatoes • Popcorn • Pigs

Book Project--_The True Story of the Three Little Pigs as Told by A. Wolf_ by John Scieszko

Read _The True Story of the Three Little Pigs as told by A. Wolf_ to your class. This book can be used for a variety of activities.

Graphing--After reading the story to your class, ask the question, "Do you believe the story the wolf told?" Record their answers on a simple yes-no bar graph.

Do you believe the story the wolf told?

Point of View--After making the bar graph, have children write why they believe or don't believe the wolf's story. It will be interesting just how many different points of view you get.

Children need practice thinking about an idea from a different perspective. Provide many opportunities to encourage this type of thinking. For example, read another pig book to the children or branch off and bring in some other fairy tales. Have the children rewrite the story or fairy tale from a different character's point of view. Or use a story such as _The Pain and the Great One_ by Judy Blume to illustrate how different people (brothers and sisters in this case) see the same situation in entirely different ways.

Interviews--Have children work in pairs to develop a list of interview questions they would ask the wolf (or another fairy tale character) and what they think his/her answers would be. They then determine who will be the wolf/character and who will ask the questions so they can present the interview to the class.

Book Project--*Charlotte's Web* by E. B. White

Charlotte's Web is a wonderful book to lead into Pig Week! Count the chapters and plan how long it will take you to read this book to your class. Plan to finish on a Friday and begin your celebration on Monday!

Sequence Murals--Discuss which events occurred in the beginning of the story, in the middle, and in the end. Divide your class into several groups. Each group will be responsible for creating a mural illustrating an event from the beginning, the middle, and the end of the story. Provide each group with a large piece of light colored butcher paper (3 yards or 3 meters long).

1. Divide your paper into three spaces.

(beginning)	(middle)	(end)

2. Decide who will work on each space. Use a variety of materials to draw your pictures.

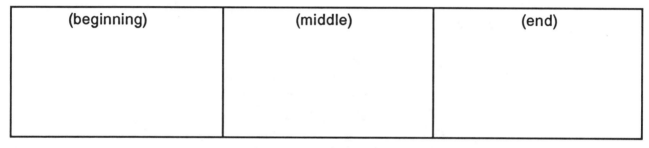

3. Write a summary for each section of your group's mural. (The higher the grade level, the more detailed the summary should be.)

Display the finished murals around the room so groups can compare and contrast the results. The murals lend themselves to the Whole Language concept of "reading the room." Children need the opportunity to read a wide variety of material in as many different formats as possible.

Letter Writing--Most children know what the word "salutations" means because of Charlotte. Take advantage of this one word to practice letter writing skills. Have the children write letters to Mr. Zuckerman asking him to spare Wilbur from an untimely death. Or children may write a letter from Charlotte or Wilbur's point of view to Fern, her family, or Mr. Zuckerman. This is what Whole Language is all about! So get those creative juices flowing.

"Positive" Webs--Charlotte saved Wilbur from an untimely death by writing positive words about her best barnyard friend. Use this activity to get children thinking positively about themselves and others.

Give each child a piece of black construction paper and white chalk. Have them draw a web on the piece of paper with the chalk. Ask them to think of one or two words that say something positive about themselves and write it on their web. These make a wonderful display and a fun activity with everyone trying to guess who each web describes. (Or have each child draw someone else's name and make a web for that person.)

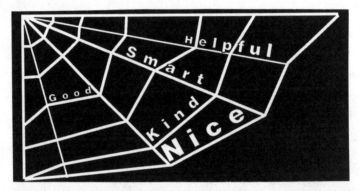

You could also make a "class web." Make a very large web out of black butcher paper. Draw in the lines of the web and have each child write one or two words about themselves on it. (This is a Pig Week celebration but this could also work into a spider unit!)

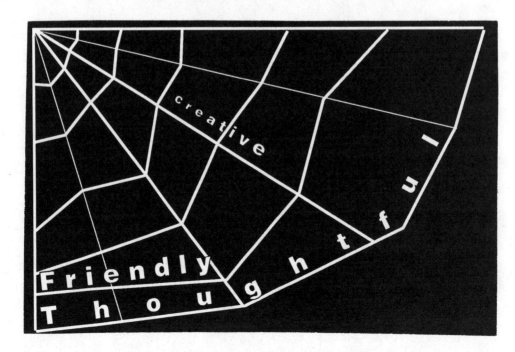

PIG MATH

Money:

"Pig Week" is the perfect time to teach or review recognizing and using money. Make piggy banks and go Hog Wild!

Make piggy banks from plain, white bleach bottles. Spread the word that you need them and have kids bring them from home. Before you start this activity with the children, rinse out the bottles thoroughly and dry them. Cut a slit in the top of the bank. Make sure it is big enough for coins and paper money to easily go through. Finish the bank in one of the following ways:

Paint the Bank--Use tempera to which liquid detergent has been added (so it will stick to the plastic). When the paint has dried, add lace or ribbon around the neck. Of course, you may all want to use the perfect PIG color...PINK!

Permanent Marking Pens--Decorate your pig with permanent marker in polka-dots, plaid, stripes, flowers, etc. Encourage children to think about their designs before beginning and not to leave too much white plastic bottle showing.

Fabric Scraps--Provide a wide variety of colors and patterns. Cut the fabric into squares. Provide watered down white glue to attach the fabric to the plastic bottle.

Eyes, Ears, Tails--Ears can be made from felt or construction paper. Eyes can be painted on or the wiggly ones from a craft store can be used. Fat pipe-cleaners make perfect curly tails for your pigs.

Use the piggy bank to show children the importance of saving money. Teach older children how to calculate interest. Reproduce the coins and bills on the following page. Give each child a set amount of money at the beginning of the week (probably coins with younger children, coins and bills with older students). Charge for certain services, such as borrowing pencils or for using the pencil sharpener more than once a day. Make a chart listing services and the basic charge for each one. Children learn very quickly the value of a dollar when you make the money learning experience real.

                   • Potatoes • Popcorn • Pigs

42 • Potatoes • Popcorn • Pigs

Counting: "My Penny Book"--Have young children just learning about money and numbers make a "piggy bank book" following these directions:

Using the pig pattern below, make 10 pages plus a cover for each child. Have the children write the numeral and the number word on each page. Provide a penny stamp and have the child stamp the correct number of pennies to correspond with the number. (If you do not have penny stamps, reproduce paper pennies for them to cut and paste.) Staple the pages together on the left.

• Potatoes • Popcorn • Pigs

"Marshmallow Pig" Math:

These charming pigs can be used for practicing numbers or for simple addition. (They could also be used for multiplication as described below.) This is a great math activity and fun to eat! (Make sure you have extra marshmallows!)

You will need:

- Pages of pink circles about 1 1/2" in diameter (1.27 cm).
- Small marshmallows
- Black marking pen

Give each child a sheet of construction paper that has been divided into two, four, or six spaces. (The size of each space will depend on how many pigs must be placed in each box to solve the problem.) Follow these steps:

1. Glue a small marshmallow on the pink circle for the body and head.
2. Use a marker to add the eyes, ears, and nostrils.
3. Glue a small marshmallow on top of the large marshmallow. This becomes the pig's snout. Add nostrils with the marker.
4. Glue a pink circle (head) on your paper.

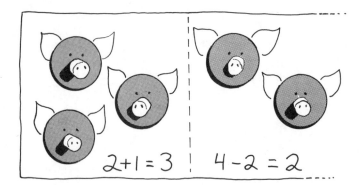

Using "marshmallow pigs":

Students are to write a numeral or an addition problem in each space. They then make and paste an appropriate number of pigs in each space to show the answer.

If you are doing this with older children, try multiplication on large sheets of paper. Divide your class into cooperative learning groups and assign each a different number. If one group has multiplication facts for four, they will make four pigs, glue them down to represent one row of four, and write 1x4=4. They will then make eight pigs and glue them down to represent two rows of four and beside them write 2x4=8 and so on. This makes a clear representation of the multiplication facts. You should do some kind of object representation and display it around the room each time you introduce a new family of multiplication facts. This enables children to see the facts and better understand this abstract concept.

 • Potatoes • Popcorn • Pigs

Estimation and Counting:

Fill a jar with plastic pigs (they can be found at cake decorating stores). Let children examine a few of the pigs to get an idea of how much space one takes up. Have the children estimate how many pigs there are in the jar. The person who is the most nearly correct wins a pig present! (Try to find an inexpensive stuffed pig for the prize or let that child spend all afternoon in the Pig Pen with a partner.)

Use the same jar of pigs to practice counting by ones, twos, threes, fives and tens. Cut off brown lunch bags, draw on fences, and have the children count the pigs into the bags. This makes a great center or a hands-on math activity.

Charlotte's Math Webs

(You may want to do this activity when reading *Charlotte's Web* to your class.)

Directions:
Write problems on the chalkboard for children to copy. Have children follow these steps.
1. Fold a piece of paper into six boxes. Write one problem in each box.
2. Draw a spider web in one corner of each box.
3. Use an ink pad to "fingerprint" the correct number of spiders on the web or coming down from the web. Add legs and eyes with a pencil or black crayon.

You may want to add a blank pig from page 47 in each square.

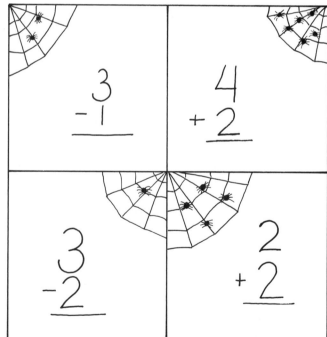

BEHAVIOR REWARDS

Make each child a "pig pen" from brown construction paper. Cut out pigs from pink construction paper. When a child is on task, helping others, etc., reward the good behavior with one of the pigs (to be glued to the pig pen). When five pigs are in the pen, reward the child with a treat (pink jelly beans) or some extra time (reading in the library, center time).

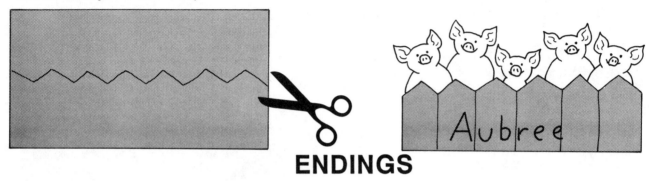

ENDINGS

The perfect ending to a week full of Pig Participation, Hog Wild Happenings, and Sow Celebrating is a Pig Out Picnic!

Have everyone in the class bring their lunch to school on Friday or the last day of "Pig Week." Ask them to be sure to include some pig products in their lunch. Ham and hotdogs would be great! Pork skins, Pigs in a Blanket...be creative and give the children several suggestions. Pass out white lunch bags and have the children decorate them appropriately for the picnic. Of course, no pig picnic would be complete without pig punch (pink lemonade).

When you have finished lunch, act out The Three Pigs. Make simple scenery on butcher paper or cardboard boxes using poster paint. If you're really ambitious, make pig and wolf masks. Let everyone take turns playing the different parts.

Children look forward to "Pig Week" each year and you will find them asking on the very first day of school..."When do we get to have 'Pig Week'?" You can't ask for a better recommendation for a week full of fun and learning!

Use these pigs for projects in this book.

47

Pleasurable "P" Activities

Use these activities when working with your Potatoes, Popcorn, or Pig units. OR... just study "P" things incorporating your favorite elements from those units into a "Preposterous P's" unit.

Fun with "P" words--Make a capital "P" out of purple butcher paper and a lower case "p" out of pink. Have students brainstorm to list all the "P" words they can think of. Use a purple marker to write on the pink paper and pink chalk to write on the purple paper. Divide the children into cooperative learning groups to sort the words by categories (food, buildings, places, animals, occupations, etc.). Leave the lists up so you can add more words as the week goes on. Why, you might even find them sneaking to the dictionary to look up more "P" words!

Picks and puffs--Give every child in your classroom two styrofoam plates and a supply of "picks" (toothpicks) and "puffs" (miniature marshmallows). Students anchor the toothpicks in the styrofoam plates when they begin building their "Picks and Puffs Palace." They build by putting the picks into the puffs, continuing to build until they have completed their palace as they envision it. The older the child the more complex the building.

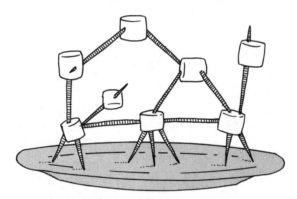

Eat a "P"--Brainstorm to create a list of "P" foods. Have a "Tasting Day" so children can experience as many of these foods as possible. For example, you might have...

Plums	Pepperoni Pizza	Potatoes	Pretzels
Peanuts	Pudding	Pita Bread	Pancakes
Pickles	Popcorn	Persimmons	Peas

Practice Alliteration Perfectly--With all these "P" words around your classroom, this is the perfect place to practice ALLITERATION. Have children listen carefully as you read some tongue twisters to see if they notice what is the same about all of them. (Hopefully they will notice that many of the words in the sentences begin with the same letter.) Give them five minutes to write a sentence using as many "P" words as possible. (With "P" words all over the place in your classroom this should be easy.) When they have the HANG of alliteration, give each child a different letter. Ask them to write as many words as they can that begin with their letter. Children will go to books, dictionaries, and each other to come up with words. Now they can practice their alliteration skill with the other letters of the alphabet.